PHARM

THINGS Y
(QUESTIC

By Rumi Michael Leigh

Introduction

I would like to thank and congratulate you for purchasing this book, " *Pharmacology, things you should know (questions and answers)*" series.

This book will help you understand, revise and have a general knowledge and keywords in Pharmacology.

Thanks again for purchasing this book, I hope you enjoy it!

Chapter 1

1) What is pharmacology ?

- Pharmacology is the study of drugs.

2) What is pharmacy ?

- Pharmacy is the art of preparation and distribution of drugs.

3) What is a drug ?

- A drug is any substance that has a pharmacological action on the body.

4) What is a curative drug ?

- A curative drug is a drug that treats infection.

5) Give an example of a curative drug.

- An antibiotic is a curative drug.

6) What is a supportive drug ?

- A supportive drug is a drug that supports and helps the body until the body recovers.

7) Give an example of a supportive drug.

- Paracetamol is a supportive drug.

8) What is a symptomatic drug ?

- A symptomatic drug is a drug that alleviates the symptoms of an infection.

9) Give examples symptomatic drugs.

- Analgesics are symptomatic drugs.

10) Do symptomatic drugs work on infections ?

- No, symptomatic drugs do not work on infections.

Chapter 2

1) What is a substitute drug ?

- A substitute drug is a drug that helps the body replace what it cannot synthesize anymore.

2) Give an example of a substitute drug.

- Insulin is an example of a substitute drug.

3) What is an analeptic drug ?

- An analeptic drug is a drug that helps the body recover.

4) Give examples of analeptic drugs.

- Vitamin supplements are examples of analeptic drugs.

5) What is the active ingredient in a drug ?

- The active ingredient is the substance that produces a pharmacological effect of a drug.

6) Give an example of an active ingredient.

- An example of an active ingredient is Paracetamol.

7) What is the simplest route to administer medications ?

- The simplest route to administer medications is the oral route.

8) What is the most common route for drug administration ?

- The most common route for drug administration is the oral route.

9) Is the oral route sufficient in a case of emergency?

- No, the oral route is not sufficient in a case of emergency.

10) What is the safest route to administer a drug in case of overdose ?

- The safest way to administer a drug in case of overdose is the oral route.

Chapter 3

1) What is pharmacodynamics ?

- Pharmacodynamics is the action of a drug on the body.

2) What is pharmacokinetics ?

- Pharmacokinetics is the action of the body on the drug.

3) What is absorption ?

- Absorption is the entry of a drug into the blood or lymph.

4) What can influence the rate of drug resorption ?

- The rate of drug resorption is influenced by gastric emptying and intestinal transit.

5) How long does it take for the stomach to be empty ?

- It takes about two hours for the stomach to be empty.

6) What can happen to the effects of a drug if it is taken at the same time with food ?

- If a drug is taken at the same time with food, it may reduce or enhance the effects of the drug.

7) What allows the distribution of drugs in the body?

- Blood circulation and intestinal tissue allow the distribution of drugs in the body.

8) What is liberation ?

- Liberation is the separation of the active ingredient of a drug.

9) What is an analgesic ?

- An analgesic is a substance, a drug which diminishes, calms, or suppresses pain.

10) At what time is it advisable to give painkillers ?

- It is advisable to give painkillers at the same time of the day.

11) What is an antipyretic ?

- An antipyretic is a medicine that reduces fever and has an anti-inflammatory effect.

Chapter 4

1) What is an agonist drug ?

- An agonist drug is a drug that produces a pharmacological action by interacting with a cellular receptor.

2) What is an antagonist drug ?

- An antagonist drug is a drug that does not produce a pharmacological action by interacting with a cellular receptor.

3) How long does it take between the administration of antagonist drugs ?

- It takes a minimum of two hours between the administration of antagonist drugs.

4) What is the antagonist of paracetamol ?

- N-acetylcysteine is the antagonist of paracetamol.

5) What are the pharmacological effects of morphine and its derivatives ?

- The pharmacological effects of morphine and its derivatives are that they are powerful analgesics, sedatives, can cause respiratory depression, constipation, etc.

6) What is the antagonist of morphine ?

- Naloxone is the antagonist of morphine.

7) Compare the analgesic effect of codeine to morphine.

- Morphine is about 10 times stronger than codeine.

8) Does morphine have a diuretic or an antidiuretic effect ?

- Morphine has an antidiuretic effect.

9) What are the side effects of morphine ?

- The side effects of morphine are nausea, vomiting, bradycardia, low blood pressure, respiratory depression, withdrawal, etc.

10) What is the action duration of codeine ?

- The action duration of codeine is about 4 to 6 hours.

Chapter 5

1) What are the side effects of codeine ?

- The side effects of codeine are dizziness, nausea, sleep disorders, bronchospasm, dry mouth, etc.

2) What are the side effects of Naloxone ?

- The side effects of Naloxone are weight gain, orthostatic hypotension, constipation, etc.

3) What do mineralocorticoid secrete ?

- Mineralocorticoid secrete aldosterone.

4) What do glucocorticoid secrete ?

- Glucocorticoids secrete cortisol.

5) How are glucocorticoids made ?

- Glucocorticoids are made by physical exercises, stress, etc.

Chapter 6

1) What is the main organ of drug metabolism ?

- The liver is the main organ of drug metabolism.

2) What limits the distribution of drugs in the central nervous system ?

- The distribution of drugs in the central nervous system is limited by the blood-brain barrier.

3) What is the half-life of a drug ?

- The half-life of a drug is the time that the concentration of a drug decreases by half.

4) How is the blood-brain barrier in children ?

- The blood-brain barrier in children is open.

5) What is an acute pain ?

- An acute pain is a short and intense pain.

6) What is a circadian rhythm ?

- A circadian rhythm means 24 hours.

Chapter 7

1) What is a generic drug ?

- A generic drug is a copy of an original drug.

2) What is the procedure of making a generic drug ?

- To be able to make a generic drug, the patent of the original drug has to be expired.

3) What is the main similarity between a generic and an original drug ?

- The main similarity between a generic and an original drug is that the active ingredients have the same amount of dose.

4) What is the main difference between a generic drug and an original drug ?

- The main difference between a generic drug and an original drug is that the excipients are different.

5) Is the excipient of a drug active ?

- No, the excipient of a drug is pharmacologically inactive.

6) Name some common excipients.

- Some common excipients are aspartame, sucrose, flavors, and lactose.

7) What are the functions of preservatives ?

- Preservatives are antioxidants and antimicrobials.

Chapter 8

1) What is galenic ?

- Galenic is the presentation of a drug in its usable form and its preparation.

2) What is an advantage of liquid forms of drugs ?

- An advantage of liquid forms of drugs is that they are easy to take.

3) What is a disadvantage of liquid forms of drugs ?

- A disadvantage of liquid forms of drugs is that they can easily be contaminated.

4) What is an advantage of solid forms of drugs ?

- An advantage of solid forms of drugs is that they can be kept for a long time.

5) What is the reference route for drug administration and why ?

- The reference route for drug administration is the intravenous route because the whole dose enters the blood.

6) When is an orodispersible used ?

- An orodispersible is used when a person has difficulty swallowing.

7) Where is an orodispersible medicine placed ?

- An orodispersible medicine is placed on the tongue.

8) Where is a sublingual medicine placed ?

- A sublingual medicine is placed under the tongue.

Chapter 9

1) Why should delayed release drugs not be crushed ?

- Delayed release and extended release drugs should not be crushed as they may delay or prolong the release of the active ingredients.

2) Why should tablets not be cut in advance ?

- Tablets should not be cut in advance because of the risk of instability of the active ingredients.

3) What causes the instability of active ingredients ?

- The instability of active ingredients can be caused by light, humidity, and air.

4) What is the normal time of capsule disintegration?

- The normal time of capsule disintegration is less than 30 minutes.

5) What is the normal time of disintegration of an effervescent drug ?

- The normal time of disintegration of an effervescent drug is less than five minutes.

6) What is a pre-scored drug ?

- Pre-scored is a drug that can be split.

7) Does a scoring line on a drug mean that you can split the drug in half ?

- No, a scoring line on a drug does not always mean that you can split a drug in half.

Chapter 10

1) How long does it take for an intravenous absorption ?

- An intravenous absorption is immediate.

2) What can cause the risk of infection when a drug is taken intravenously ?

- The injection can cause an infection when a drug is taken intravenously.

3) What can cause toxic risks when a drug is taken intravenously ?

- The drug itself can cause toxic risks when taken intravenously.

4) How long does it take for the absorption of an intramuscular drug ?

- For an intramuscular drug, the absorption is between 10 to 20 minutes.

5) Give a disadvantage of the absorption of an intramuscular drug.

- A disadvantage of the absorption of an intramuscular drug is pain.

6) Give a disadvantage of an intra-arterial drug absorption.

- A disadvantage of the absorption of an intra-arterial drug is spasm.

7) How long does it take for an absorption of a subcutaneous drug ?

- For a subcutaneous drug, the absorption is between 15 to 30 minutes.

8) Give an advantage of pulmonary drug absorption.

- An advantage of pulmonary drug absorption is its rapid absorption.

9) Why is there a rapid absorption of medications by the pulmonary route ?

- There is a rapid absorption of medications by the pulmonary route because there is rich vascularization.

Chapter 11

1) What is NSAID ?

- Nonsteroidal anti-inflammatory drug.

2) How does NSAIDs work ?

- NSAIDs act by inhibiting prostaglandins and thromboxane.

3) Can NSAIDs cause headaches ?

- Yes, NSAIDs can cause headaches.

4) What are the risks of using aspirin ?

- The risks of using aspirin are bleeding, ulcer, and perforation.

Chapter 12

1) What is the function of cyclooxygenase ?

- Cyclooxygenase is involved in the formation of prostaglandin.

2) What is the function of prostaglandin in the inflammatory process ?

- Prostaglandin has a vasodilator function during the inflammatory process.

3) What is the function of prostaglandin during childbirth ?

- Prostaglandin stimulates contractions during childbirth.

4) How do prostaglandins protect the gastric mucosa ?

- Prostaglandins protect the gastric mucosa by increasing mucus production and decreasing the secretion of hydrochloric acid.

Chapter 13

1) Is there a peripheral anti-inflammatory action of paracetamol ?

- No, there is no peripheral anti-inflammatory action of paracetamol.

2) Is there an anti-aggregating action of paracetamol on platelets ?

- No, there is no anti-aggregating action of paracetamol on platelets.

3) Is there an ulcerogenic action of paracetamol ?

- No, there is no ulcerogenic action of paracetamol.

4) Where does the main action of paracetamol occur ?

- The main action of paracetamol occurs in the central nervous system.

5) How does paracetamol reduce pain and fever without anti-inflammatory and antiplatelet activities ?

- Paracetamol reduces pain and fever without anti-inflammatory and antiplatelet activities by inhibiting cerebral cox 3.

6) What are the side effects of paracetamol ?

- The side effects of paracetamol are kidney failure, bronchospasm, allergy, etc.

Chapter 14

1) What is another name for cortisol ?

- Another name for cortisol is hydrocortisone.

2) What are the side effects of cortisol ?

- The side effects of cortisol are muscle atrophy, an increase in blood sugar, osteoporosis, etc.

3) Does cortisol degrade proteins into amino acids in the liver ?

- No, cortisol does not degrade proteins into amino acids in the liver.

4) Does cortisol increase or decrease cardiac output?

- Cortisol increases cardiac output.

5) What are the functions of corticosteroids ?

- Corticosteroids are anti-inflammatory and antiallergics.

6) What can happen during an abrupt withdrawal of corticosteroids ?

- An abrupt withdrawal of corticosteroids can lead to adrenal insufficiency.

7) Are corticosteroids injectable ?

- Yes, corticosteroids are injectable intravenously and intramuscularly.

8) Are there other routes of the administration of corticosteroids ?

- Yes, there are other routes of the administration of corticosteroids that include oral, inhalers, creams, etc.

9) Can corticosteroids mask signs of infection ?

- Yes, corticosteroids can mask signs of infection.

10) How can corticosteroids cause osteoporosis ?

- Corticosteroids can cause osteoporosis by the breakdown of bone proteins.

11) How can corticosteroids help after transplanting an organ ?

- Corticosteroids can help after an organ transplantation by preventing transplant rejection.

Conclusion

Thank you again for purchasing this book. I hope it has helped you in your journey to understanding Pharmacology.

Thank you.

Printed in Great Britain
by Amazon

70341905R00017